Disney Fairies

Prilla
and the
Butterfly
Lie

Prilla
and the
Butterfly
Lie

WRITTEN BY
KITTY RICHARDS

ILLUSTRATED BY
DENISE SHIMABUKURO
& THE DISNEY STORYBOOK ARTISTS

HarperCollins *Children's Books*

First published in the USA by Disney Press,
114 Fifth Avenue, New York, New York, 10011-5690.

First published in Great Britain in 2006
by HarperCollins Children's Books.
HarperCollins Children's Books is a division of
HarperCollins Publishers,
77 - 85 Fulham Palace Road, Hammersmith, London, W6 8JB.

The HarperCollins Children's Books website is
www.harpercollinschildrensbooks.co.uk

978-0-00-721400-6
0-00-721400-6

1 2 3 4 5 6 7 8 9 10

Printed and bound in the UK

Visit disneyfairies.com

This book is proudly printed on paper which contains wood
from well managed forests, certified in accordance with
the rules of the Forest Stewardship Council.
For more information about FSC,
please visit www.fsc-uk.org

Mixed Sources
Product group from well-managed
forests and other controlled sources
www.fsc.org Cert no. SW-COC-1806
© 1996 Forest Stewardship Council
FSC

All About Fairies

IF YOU HEAD toward the second star on your right and fly straight on till morning, you'll come to Never Land, a magical island where mermaids play and children never grow up.

When you arrive, you might hear something like the tinkling of little bells. Follow that sound and you'll find Pixie Hollow, the secret heart of Never Land.

A great old maple tree grows in Pixie Hollow, and in it live hundreds of fairies and sparrow men. Some of them can do water magic, others can fly like the wind, and still others can speak to animals. You see, Pixie Hollow is the Never fairies' kingdom, and each fairy who lives there has a special, extraordinary talent.

Not far from the Home Tree, nestled in the branches of a hawthorn, is Mother Dove, the most magical creature of all. She sits on her egg, watching over the fairies, who in turn watch over her. For as long as Mother Dove's egg stays well and whole, no one in Never Land will ever grow old.

Once, Mother Dove's egg *was* broken. But we are not telling the story of the egg here. Now it is time for Prilla's tale…

Prilla
and the
Butterfly
Lie

1

PRILLA KNELT ON the library shelf. She put her hands over her mouth to hold back her laughter. She kept her eyes on a little girl in pigtails who stood on her tiptoes, reaching for a book.

The girl grabbed the book and slid it off the shelf. Quick as a wink, Prilla popped out from the space where the book had been. The little girl stared at Prilla for a moment. Then she squealed with delight, her blue eyes wide.

"A fairy!"

"Shhh!" said the librarian. She gave the girl a stern look. Prilla giggled. She turned a somersault in the air and…

"Grab him, Prilla!" a voice cried.

Suddenly, Prilla was in a sunny meadow, back in Pixie Hollow. Nettle, a caterpillar-shearing-talent fairy, stood in front of her, holding a pair of shears. Nettle pointed to the caterpillar that Prilla was supposed to be keeping still. The caterpillar was bucking around like a little green bronco. It had knocked over a sack of caterpillar fuzz. Prilla was ankle-deep in the stuff.

Prilla sighed. It had been a long and trying day. She was very fond of Nettle, who enjoyed games as much as she did.

Just the week before, Prilla and Nettle had had a cartwheel race across a field of buttercups. Afterward, they had collapsed in the grass in a fit of giggles. That was when Nettle had asked her if she would like to give caterpillar shearing a try. Prilla had agreed.

The day had started well enough. Nettle gave Prilla a tour of the caterpillar corral. First they had seen some caterpillars hatching from eggs. Then they'd watched a few caterpillars shedding their skin. Next they had seen some furry caterpillars making their cocoons.

Suddenly, Nettle had grabbed Prilla's arm. "We're just in time to watch a butterfly hatch!" she'd whispered.

Prilla had held her breath as they'd silently watched the butterfly emerge from its cocoon. She was amazed that a funny-looking caterpillar could transform into such a beautiful creature.

Watching the butterfly hatch had been exciting. But Prilla had quickly realised that shearing caterpillars was not. Her job was to hold the caterpillars while Nettle clipped their fuzz with her shears. Prilla tried hard to help. But the truth was that she didn't really like shearing caterpillars at all. It was hot in the sun. It was dull doing the same thing over and over again. But most of all, Prilla just didn't like caterpillars. Not one bit. They were prickly. They were kind of ugly. And they were ornery.

Bored, Prilla had finally allowed herself to drift off and blink over to the mainland. Prilla was a mainland-visiting clapping-talent fairy, the only one in Pixie Hollow. In the blink of an eye, she could zip from Never Land to the mainland to visit children. Prilla's talent was very important, for it kept children's belief in fairies alive. When children didn't believe in them, fairies died.

But Prilla didn't visit the mainland only to save fairies' lives. She also went because it was her favourite thing in the world to do.

And look what had happened! She hadn't been paying attention, and now things were getting out of control.

Prilla leaned forward to grab the cranky caterpillar around its middle. It wiggled away from her, and Prilla stumbled. The other shearing-talent fairies chuckled in sympathy.

"He's a wild one, he is," said Jason, a caterpillar-shearing-talent sparrow man.

Prilla tried once again to seize the creature. The caterpillar reared up. Prilla lost her balance and fell backward. She landed in the grass with a soft thump.

"Don't worry, Prilla. You can do it!" Jason called, noticing the frown on Prilla's face.

Still the restless caterpillar wiggled. "There, there," said Nettle in a soothing voice. She put down her shears.

Nettle's gentle tone calmed the caterpillar. It began to settle down. Prilla stood and brushed herself off. Not knowing what else to do, she bent to pat the caterpillar on the head.

Quickly, Nettle began to shear the caterpillar. In a couple of minutes, she was done. "That wasn't so bad, was it?" she asked.

Prilla wasn't sure if Nettle was talking to her or to the caterpillar. She shook her head anyway.

Nettle let the newly shorn caterpillar go. Prilla watched as it inched away as fast as it could – which was pretty slow.

Nettle smiled at Prilla. "You sit and rest," she said. "I'll do the cleaning up."

Prilla lowered herself onto a moss-covered stone. She picked a stray piece of caterpillar fuzz from the hem of her pale pink silk skirt. Nettle and the other caterpillar shearers began sweeping up the loose fuzz.

Thank goodness that's over, Prilla thought. *Maybe tomorrow I won't do anything but blink over to the mainland as many times as I want.* It would be a perfect day.

Nettle put the caterpillar fuzz she'd swept up into a sack made of woven grass. She tied it shut with a flourish. Then she loaded it onto a wheelbarrow full of sacks.

Jason picked up the handles of the wheelbarrow. He set off with the load toward the Home Tree, the towering maple tree where the fairies lived and worked. "Have fun, Prilla. Thanks for your help!" he cried.

"Fly safely, Jason!" said Prilla. She waved.

Nettle sat next to her on the stone and patted Prilla's knee. "What a great day," Nettle said. "I could tell how much you enjoyed it."

"Well, I – " Prilla began.

"Being outside, working with those wonderful caterpillars." Nettle leaned in close to Prilla. She lowered her voice as if she were about to tell her a secret. "Other talents might argue with me, but caterpillar shearing really is the most important talent. Wouldn't you agree?"

She went on, not waiting for Prilla to answer. "First of all, it helps the caterpillars grow nice woolly coats for when it's time to build their cocoons. And then there're all the great things we make out of the fuzz!" She began to list them on her fingers. "Soft pillows, cosy comforters, light-as-a-feather blankets, thick sweaters, those wonderful linens… " Her voice trailed off.

Prilla nodded. She liked pillows,

comforters, blankets, sweaters, and linens as much as the next fairy did. It seemed that caterpillar shearing was indeed very important.

"Yes, it is a lovely talent," she said out loud. *I just hope I never have to help shear another caterpillar ever again!* she silently added. She leaned back on her elbows.

And before Prilla knew it, she had blinked over to the mainland. She saw a little girl holding a fluffy white dandelion. The girl pursed her lips to blow the seeds. Prilla flew toward her…

"I said, what do you think?" Nettle said suddenly.

Prilla started. Nettle was looking at her expectantly.

"Sorry, can you repeat that?" Prilla asked.

And then Nettle said the dreaded words: "Same time tomorrow?"

2

PRILLA'S HEART SANK. She stared at Nettle's hopeful face. *No, thank you,* she said in her head. *I have other plans. I don't like caterpillars. I don't like them at all.* She just didn't say the words out loud.

"Why, sure," Prilla found herself saying. "I'd be happy to help you out again."

"Great!" said Nettle. "I knew you'd love my talent as much as I do!"

Nettle stood and picked up the last sack of caterpillar fuzz. She slung it over her shoulder and headed back to the Home Tree, whistling merrily.

Well, that didn't go very well, Prilla thought. *And it certainly changes my plans for tomorrow!* She'd have to blink over to the mainland that night after dinner instead.

As she got up to leave, the still evening air was stirred by a sudden brisk breeze. Out of the corner of her eye, Prilla saw a flash of purple. And there, standing in front of her, was Vidia.

"Hello, dearest," said Vidia. "Did you have a nice day today? Do something fun?" Her tone was mocking, as usual.

"Well, I – " Prilla began.

"Come, darling. Let's go for a walk, shall we?" Without waiting for Prilla's response, Vidia set off at a quick pace.

Prilla stared at Vidia's retreating back in confusion. As the fastest of the fast-flying-talent fairies, Vidia never walked when she could fly. It went against her nature.

What is going on? Prilla wondered. She followed Vidia to find out, racing to catch up. Even on land, Vidia was fast.

Finally, Vidia came to a stop at the edge of a minnow pond. It was nearly sunset, and the sky was a soft shade of pinkish purple. There was a pleasant chorus of chirping crickets and peeping frogs. Fireflies had begun lighting up the dusky air around them.

Vidia turned to face Prilla. "So what have you been up to lately, dearest?" she asked.

"Oh, a little of this, a little of that," Prilla answered.

"Mmm-hmm," replied Vidia. She had a funny look on her face, as if she was trying not to smirk. "A little tree-bark grading?" Vidia asked sweetly.

Prilla nodded. She remembered the splinters she had gotten that day.

"Maybe some floor polishing?" Vidia went on.

Prilla winced. She had spent an entire afternoon on her hands and knees, helping polish the mica entryway in the Home Tree.

"And some dandelion-fluff sorting?"

"That made me sneeze," Prilla recalled. She was beginning to feel self-conscious. Had she *really* been spending that much time helping out other talents?

"Not to mention the time you helped the ink-making-talent fairies."

Prilla glanced down at her hands. If she looked closely, she could still see some of the purple ink under her fingernails and in the wrinkly skin around her knuckles.

She cleared her throat to speak. But Vidia wasn't through.

"And then a little caterpillar shearing today… Look, Prilla," Vidia said. She put her hands on her hips. "I've been trying to ignore it, but your nicey-nice behavior is getting on my last nerve. I've got a new talent for you, sweetness – doormat talent. You let everyone walk all over you."

Prilla cringed. Was she really that bad?

"Don't look at me as if I've been pulling the wings off dragonflies. I know everyone around here thinks I'm horrible, but I do try to help out a fellow fairy now and then. So I'm helping you now. I don't want to see you hurt."

Vidia scowled fiercely. Prilla had the feeling Vidia hadn't meant to say that last part.

Raising her chin, Vidia flipped her hair back and said, "Face it, Prilla, you've got a problem."

"A problem? What do you mean, Vidia?" asked Prilla.

"You are the fairy who just can't say no."

Prilla stared at her shoes. "Well, what's wrong with being helpful?" she asked, a little defensively.

She didn't want to say it out loud to Vidia, but she *liked* it when other fairies asked her for help. In Pixie Hollow, talent groups did everything together. They worked together, played together, ate their meals together. When Prilla had first arrived, she hadn't known what her talent was. She had felt very alone.

Prilla had desperately wanted to fit in back then. In the end, she'd found her talent and her place among the fairies. But even now, every time someone asked for her help, she felt glad.

She knew that Vidia would never understand. Vidia was a loner. She preferred her own company to that of anyone else. Why, she even lived alone in a sour-plum tree, apart from the rest of the fairies.

Vidia gave Prilla an exasperated look. "Sweetness, what is the only thing that's important to me?" she asked.

That wasn't hard to answer. "Flying fast, of course," Prilla replied.

"And why is that?" Vidia asked.

Prilla was puzzled. "Because you like to... fly quickly?"

Vidia rolled her eyes. "Because it's my *talent*, pumpkin. The most important thing to any fairy is her talent." She crossed her arms and smirked at Prilla. "But the most important thing to you, apparently, is being helpful!" Vidia made a disgusted face as she said the word "helpful."

With a sinking heart, Prilla realized that Vidia was right. She had been spending too much time on other fairies' talents and not enough time on her own.

"But I don't like to say no," Prilla admitted. "I don't want to hurt anyone's feelings."

"Why not just say, 'Be gone with

you! Your stupid talent bores me!'?" Vidia suggested.

Prilla gasped. "You know I could never say that!"

"Okay, okay," Vidia said. "Maybe that isn't your style. But the next time a fairy asks you to help with some dreadful task, you should say, 'Forget it. I'm not interested. I have my own talent to attend to.'"

Prilla frowned. "Why do you care, Vidia? Why do you want to help me?"

Vidia paused. Then she shrugged. "You helped me once. I'm just returning the favour."

And quick as a wink, she was gone.

Prilla walked home slowly, deep in thought. Vidia was right. Prilla was not a caterpillar-shearing fairy. She wasn't a tree-bark-grading fairy. Or an entryway-polishing fairy. Or one of any of those other talents.

Prilla was the one and only mainland-visiting clapping-talent fairy. And it was time she started acting like it.

3

THE MORNING SUNLIGHT crept into Prilla's room, waking her. She yawned and stretched.

Feeling very lazy, she located a few grains of fairy dust and, from her bed, sprinkled some on her washing-up items. Magically, the pitcher poured water – not too hot, not too cold, but just right – into the washing bowl. A velvety moss washcloth dipped itself into the warm water, wrung itself out, and gently scrubbed her face. She giggled as it washed behind her ears. It tickled.

Next she flicked a grain onto her pine needle–bristle hairbrush. Exactly twenty-five strokes later, her hair was glossy and tangle free. Prilla considered using fairy dust to get dressed. She laughed at the thought of her clothes marching out of the wardrobe and modeling themselves for her as she considered each outfit.

Instead, Prilla climbed out of bed and made her way to her closet. She took off her whisper-soft white muslin nightgown and put on her favorite pink silk dress with purple trim. After fastening its leafy green belt around her tiny waist, she began to search for her matching shoes. Finally, she found them far underneath her bed. She pulled the buckles tightly around her ankles. Now she was ready to face the day.

She skipped out of her room. In the hallway, she nearly bumped into Cinda, one of Queen Clarion's helper fairies.

"Excuse me, Cinda," Prilla said. But

Cinda seemed to be in a rush and hardly noticed.

On Prilla's way to the tearoom, her stomach rumbled. She smiled when she saw the breakfast that Dulcie and the rest of the baking-talent fairies had made. There were chocolate turnovers, acorn bread, lemon poppy-seed rolls, blueberry muffins, and cinnamon twists. There were several different spreads – honey butter, pumpkin butter, and maple butter, plus strawberry, gooseberry, chokecherry, and beach plum jams. Steaming pots of peppermint tea sat next to icy pitchers of raspberry, blueberry, and sparkling red Never berry juice on the table.

Prilla smiled again as she recalled the time she'd helped out in the kitchen. "Anyone can learn to bake!" Dulcie had insisted. After a fallen cake, a dozen rock-hard muffins, and two baking sheets of burnt, misshapen cookies, Dulcie had been forced to admit defeat. "I guess some fairies aren't meant to bake after all," she had said with a shake of her head.

Prilla scanned the room, looking for a place to sit. It was a busy morning in the tearoom. She thought she'd like to catch up with her friend Rani, but the water-talent table was full. So was the pots-and-pans-talent table, so she couldn't sit with Tinker Bell, either. She saw an empty chair at the garden-talent table, where her friend Lily was sitting. But then Rosetta took the seat. Finally, Prilla spotted an open place at the decoration-talent table and headed toward it.

"Yoo-hoo! Prilla!" called a familiar voice. Nettle waved to her from across the room.

Oh, no, Prilla thought. She had planned to tell Nettle the bad news *after* breakfast. But then she shrugged. *I might as well get it over with,* she thought. She took a deep breath andheaded toward the caterpillar shearers table.

"Our honourary caterpillar shearer!" gushed Jason. "We're looking forward to working with you again today."

Nettle patted the seat next to her. "Sit down," she said. She noticed Prilla hesitate. "What's the matter, Prilla?" she asked.

Now was the perfect time to tell her. But Prilla didn't know how to begin.

"Are you ill?" Nettle asked.

Prilla shook her head. She gulped. "Actually, I have to be honest with you, Nettle," she said.

"Yes?" said Nettle. Her hazel eyes widened.

"Here's the thing about caterpillars… ," Prilla began. She opened her mouth to say, "I don't like them." But nothing came out. She couldn't say the words aloud.

Nettle smiled. "I know," she said. "Aren't they great?"

Prilla lost her nerve. "Yes," she fibbed. "Caterpillars *are* great." Then she had an idea. "But there's something I like even better."

"What is it?" asked Nettle. "What could possibly be even better than caterpillars?"

Prilla bit her lip. Her mind was a complete blank. "I like... " She frantically tried to think of something. *Think, Prilla, think!* She stared out the window for inspiration.

At that moment, a pretty pink and blue butterfly flitted past. "Butterflies!" Prilla said triumphantly. "I like butterflies!" She felt relieved for a split second. Then she thought, *Butterflies? Why did I just say that?*

Nettle gave her a puzzled look. "Butterflies?" she finally said. "Are you sure?"

It was too late to change her answer now. "Yes, I'm sure," Prilla said, nodding. "Lovely butterflies. I just can't get enough of them. Such colourful, delicate creatures. They fly, you know. All over the place. Fascinating," she babbled.

"Butterflies," Nettle said. "How unusual." She shook her head, as if to clear it. "That's very… interesting." Nettle paused for a moment. "Well, I guess you won't be helping us with the caterpillars today, then?"

"I guess not," said Prilla. "I'll be focusing on… butterflies."

Nettle's brow wrinkled. "If you say so," she said.

"See you later, Nettle," said Prilla. She crossed the room and found an empty seat at the keyhole-design table. As she sat down, she braced herself for someone to ask her to help design keyholes.

But to her relief, no one did. Instead, the fairies at the table chatted about the designs they were planning to create that day. Prilla smiled and ate her breakfast in silence.

She took a big bite of a roll. Light and flaky and buttery – delicious. The jam was both tart and sweet. *Mmm*. She had forgotten how hungry she was.

As she ate, she thought about what she had told Nettle. Not being truthful to Nettle had been wrong. But Prilla had only done it to spare her friend's feelings. There was no reason to think about it anymore. It was over and done with.

That is the end of that, Prilla thought.

4

THAT EVENING AT DINNER, Prilla sat quietly by herself. She thought about all the adventures she'd had that day blinking over to the mainland. She had surprised a little girl struggling over a homework problem. She'd cheered up a boy who'd been kept after school for talking in class. She had played peekaboo with a baby, who had screamed with delight.

She had also visited a toy store, where she had amused young shoppers by sitting in the engine of a toy train. Then she'd hid behind a stack of sugar cones in an ice cream parlor. She had flown to the top of a Ferris wheel and made faces at the riders. Later, she'd sat on a little girl's shoulder at the circus while clowns tumbled and cheerful music played.

Ding, ding, ding, ding, ding! Prilla looked up to see Cinda tapping her water glass with a fork. A hush fell over the tearoom. That was the signal that Queen Clarion, the leader of all the Never fairies, had an important announcement to make.

Queen Clarion, lovely and regal, as always, swept into the room. *She seems a bit anxious,* Prilla thought, sitting up straight in her chair.

"My fellow fairies," Queen Clarion said, "I don't want to alarm anyone, but I have some rather unpleasant news to share with you this evening." She paused for a moment. "I am sorry to tell you that there has been an outbreak of fairy pox."

There was a sharp collective intake of breath.

"Several of your fellow fairies have already been infected," the queen went on.

The room began to buzz. Some of the newer fairies asked the older fairies to explain what fairy pox was. There hadn't been an outbreak of fairy pox in Pixie Hollow in many years. But it was hard to miss a fairy with the pox. The fairies who got it broke out into spots. The spots could be quite pretty – pale pink, blue, and purple. But fairy pox made fairies dangerously sleepy. A fairy could fall asleep at the table and drown in her soup bowl if she wasn't careful! Luckily, with plenty of bed rest and a daily dose of daisy pollen, fairies were almost always cured.

Over the noise, the queen said, "Fairy pox may not be life threatening, but it is very contagious. All ill fairies have been moved to the infirmary. Only nursing-talent fairies are allowed to have contact with sick fairies. So the rest of you, please keep your distance from anyone who is ill."

There was silence. The fairies began to check each other for the telltale spots.

Bess, an art-talent fairy, looked down at her paint-speckled arms. "I forgot to wash up before dinner!" she explained. The rest of the fairies at her table laughed nervously. Then they shifted away from her, just a bit.

Iris, a garden-talent fairy who had been up all night searching for a rare shrinking violet, let out a jaw-popping yawn. She was surprised when her tablemates on both sides of her hastily excused themselves and found seats at another table.

Queen Clarion looked around the room. "Are there any questions?"

"Can you tell us who is sick?" a light-talent sparrow man asked.

Queen Clarion gestured toward the nursing-talent table. "Poppy, would you like to give an update?" she asked.

Poppy, a jolly nursing-talent fairy, stood up. "There are a dozen sick fairies so far." She began listing them on her fingers. "Olivia, Heather, Flora, Marigold, Jordan, Zuzu, Amaryllis, Rhia, Aidan, Russell, Violet, and Primrose are ill," she reported. "But they are all resting comfortably. They are sleeping a lot, as you can imagine! Why, just the other night, Jordan was telling a marvelious story about a battle between Captain Hook and a sea serpent. He fell sound asleep just as he got to the best part! I was almost tempted to wake him up to see what happened next!"

Everyone laughed. Jordan was one of the finest storytelling-talent fairies.

"So you see, your friends are in good hands. They'll soon be as good as new." Poppy sat down.

Queen Clarion spoke again. "So if there are no more questions, the serving-talent fairies can bring in the first – "

"Wait! Wait!" Jason interrupted. He stood up. "It looks like each and every one of the butterfly herders is sick! All eight of them!"

Heads swung around to peer at the butterfly herders' table. Sure enough, it was empty!

A look of alarm crossed the queen's face. The butterflies were important to the fairies, since they laid the eggs that became caterpillars. If anything were to happen to the butterfly herd, the fairies wouldn't have any caterpillars – or any caterpillar fuzz.

"Well," the queen said, "I am sure we'll have no problem getting volunteers to help with the butterfly herding until they are able to return to work. Would anyone like to pitch in?" She looked around hopefully.

An uncomfortable silence filled the tearoom. Some fairies studied their forks.

Others examined their dinner plates very closely. No one would look up.

"No volunteers," said the queen. "This is indeed a problem. What are we to do?"

"I know!" said a voice. "There is a fairy who would be happy to help out. She *loves* butterflies."

The room began to buzz once more. Everyone wondered who the butterfly-loving fairy could be.

Prilla sank into her chair until her head was barely level with the table. She had completely forgotten about her butterfly lie.

"And who is this fairy?" Queen Clarion asked.

"It's Prilla!" said Nettle. "She told me she likes butterflies even better than caterpillars!" she announced.

Prilla stared at the tablecloth. Her glow turned orange as she blushed. She felt every fairy in the tearoom peering at her curiously.

Even the queen looked surprised. "Is this true, Prilla?" she asked.

Without looking up, Prilla spoke. "Yes, it's true," she said miserably. "I did tell Nettle that."

When Prilla did raise her head, she found herself looking right at Vidia, who was directly across the room. Vidia rolled her eyes and shook her head. Prilla could just imagine what she was thinking – that that silly little fairy had gone and done it again!

5

KNOCK! KNOCK! KNOCK!

"Rise and shine, Prilla! It's time to start your day!" a wake-up-talent fairy called through the door.

Prilla struggled to open her eyes. Was it morning already? Hadn't she *just* fallen asleep? The sun was not even up yet!

Butterfly-herding talents certainly start their day very early, Prilla thought. She groaned and rolled out of bed.

She was still half-asleep as she pulled a simple cotton dress over her head. She didn't even notice that she put on two different kinds of socks or that her dress was buttoned wrong.

She picked up her hairbrush. She remembered how the queen had smiled at her gratefully the night before. "Good luck tomorrow," the queen had said. "Never butterflies are beautiful creatures, my dear. But of course, they are prone to … " She stopped and shook her head. "But you know all about butterflies – you love them! You'll have no problem at all!"

Prone to what? Prilla had wanted to ask. But she couldn't let on that she didn't know anything about looking after butterflies.

Sighing, Prilla set down her hairbrush and headed downstairs.

Dulcie met Prilla at the front door, holding a small sack. She laughed when she saw Prilla's sleepy face and mismatched socks.

Dulcie handed Prilla the sack. "Your breakfast," she said.

A dust-talent fairy was waiting outside with Prilla's daily dose of fairy dust. She sprinkled a level teacup of dust – not a smidgen more or a smidgen less – over Prilla. As usual, it was shivery and cool as it settled on Prilla's head and shoulders.

"Thank you," Prilla said. She slung the sack over her shoulder, took a deep breath, and rose into the air.

The sun was coming up over the hills. The meadow was starting to buzz with the sound of insects. Prilla began to feel better. *I'm herding butterflies, not water snakes, for goodness' sake!* she told herself. *How hard can it be?*

Woods, valleys, meadows, streams, ponds, and colorful flowers all stretched out beneath her. Prilla turned a few aerial cartwheels and laughed with joy. There was something exciting about being up before everyone else. It made the day seem filled with adventure and possibility.

Prilla spied the garden-talent fairies' flower-filled gardens. She could pick out Lily's garden by the orange and red poppies, which were the biggest in Pixie Hollow. Prilla flew over the part of Havendish Stream where the water talents sometimes gathered. Looking back, she could see the Home Tree, small in the distance.

She looked down as she passed over a clearing. To her delight, she spotted the herd of butterflies!

Prilla hovered in the air, drinking in the scene. There were about fifty of the delicate creatures. Their wings beat lazily as they sunned themselves in the early-morning warmth.

And the colours! They took Prilla's breath away. There were shades of red, orange, yellow, green, blue, violet, shimmery gold, burnished copper, and shining silver. They were more beautiful than the biggest and brightest rainbow Prilla had ever seen.

The sun was barely up and she'd already found the butterflies. *Why, this is going to be easy!* Prilla smiled. She'd be done so early, she would have plenty of time for a nap and a blink over to the mainland before dinner.

Taking a deep breath, she landed quietly in the middle of the butterfly herd. That was when she realised she wasn't sure what to do next. Finding the group was one thing. But Prilla didn't know the first thing about herding them.

"Um, hello, butterflies," she said uncertainly. Prilla knew that the butterflies weren't able to understand her. But that didn't stop her from talking to them anyway. "I'll be your herder today. Our first stop will be Flower Field," she said.

Flower Field was a nearby meadow filled with wildflowers of all shapes, sizes, and colours – stately Queen Anne's lace, snappy black-eyed Susans, lovely Indian paintbrush. It seemed like a perfect place for butterflies

"So let's go!" Prilla said, clapping her hands.

And to her delight, all the butterflies

lifted off into the air!

How wonderful! Prilla thought as they rose. They began to circle. *So far so good.*

But without warning, the butterflies started to turn off in different directions. Prilla's heart sank. This wasn't how it was supposed to be!

"Hey, wait!" Prilla shouted. She chased after a blue and purple butterfly and waved her hands to get it to stay with the others.

But just as she reached it, the butterfly dropped several inches in the air. Prilla found herself headed right for a tree branch! At the last second, she ducked under it.

Just then, she noticed that a tiny silvery yellow butterfly had gotten quite far away from the others. That wouldn't do at all! Prilla took off after it and chased it back to the herd.

But the butterflies wouldn't stay together. Prilla hovered in the air, staring at them. She wondered what she was doing wrong. This was exhausting!

Suddenly, Prilla noticed that the butterflies were starting to move closer together. She watched with pleasure as they formed one large group. "That's more like it," she said.

Just as she was about to try to shepherd them to Flower Field, she realised that the herd of butterflies had started to pick up speed. They were headed right for her!

"Stop! Stop!" Prilla cried. But they kept coming, all fifty of them. It would have been beautiful if it hadn't been so frightening!

In a second, the butterflies were upon her. They surrounded her on all sides. Prilla felt the breeze from one hundred beating wings.

"Hey… wait… what are you doing?" she said. She found herself being jostled and pushed.

The next thing she knew, she felt rough tree bark against her back. Suddenly, the butterflies broke apart. Prilla was dangling from a branch high above the ground.

What happened? Prilla thought. She tried to turn around, but she couldn't. Then she understood. Her belt had gotten caught on a twig. She was stuck.

Prilla watched as the swarm of butterflies merrily flew away, flitting and fluttering. She gazed after them until they were merely a colourful band across the sky. Finally, they dis-appeared from her sight.

"This is a fine mess you've gotten yourself into, Prilla," she scolded herself.

She sighed. The ground was a long way down. Squirm as she might, she wasn't budging an inch. Butterfly herding had certainly gotten off to a disappointing start!

6

A SLIGHT BREEZE BLEW, and Prilla swayed back and forth in the air. She wondered how in the world she was going to get down. At least no one was around to see her. Thank goodness for that.

"Prilla!" someone shouted.

Oh dear, Prilla thought. *How embarassing to be caught like this!* She looked down at the ground. Pluck, a harvest-talent fairy, was staring up at her. Her hands were on her hips. Her mouth formed an O of surprise.

"Prilla! What are you doing up there?" Pluck called up.

"Oh, I'm just scouting for butterflies!" Prilla cried. She cupped her hand over her eyes and scanned the horizon. "Nope! Haven't spotted any yet! But just give me time! I'll be herding them here and there before you know it!"

Pluck flew up to hover near Prilla's branch. Prilla gulped and gave Pluck a big fake smile that was meant to say, "Things may look a bit out of the ordinary to you, but really, everything is perfectly fine."

But Pluck was having none of that. She looked closely at Prilla and frowned. "It looks to me like you're stuck!" she concluded.

Prilla laughed nervously. "Oh, no, this is my special lookout twig," she explained. "Don't you worry about me!"

She crossed her arms and smiled, even though her belt was digging into her waist. She decided to change the subject.

"So what are you up to today?" she asked, as if she and Pluck were having a pleasant talk over tea.

Pluck gave Prilla an odd look. Then she shrugged and began to explain. "There were reports of a gigantic bush full of plump, juicy blackberries near Flower Field," she said. "Have you spotted it?"

Prilla shook her head. "But I'll be sure to let you know if I do." She frowned at Pluck. Why wasn't she leaving? "So good luck finding the bush!" Prilla said enthusiastically. "Blackberries, how delicious!"

"Thanks," said Pluck. She seemed to be thinking about something. "I know! Why don't you leave your lookout twig for a while and come with me?" she suggested. "Never butterflies love berries, you know. Maybe the herd will be there. Then you can help me harvest the berries. And I can help you herd the butterflies!"

It was a good idea. Herding butterflies would be so much easier with two fairies instead of one. But Prilla couldn't move without admitting that she was stuck. And then she would have to explain the embarrassing way she had come to be stuck. As far as Prilla was concerned, that was not an option.

"Oh, it's okay," said Prilla. "I think I'll stay right here for the time being." She smiled as if she hadn't a care in the world.

"Whatever suits you," said Pluck. Then she grinned at Prilla. "Those butterflies are something else, aren't they?" she said. "I have so much respect for the butterfly talents. We were all so happy when you volunteered!"

She leaned over and gave Prilla a playful tap on the shoulder. Prilla swung gently from side to side. "You are one brave fairy!" Pluck said.

Prilla's eyes widened. Brave? What did Pluck mean? But to ask would be the same as saying, "I have no idea what you are talking about. And that's because I told a lie to Nettle – and to the queen!" So Prilla just laughed uneasily. She mumbled a farewell. And Pluck, with one backward glance at Prilla, finally took off. A short while later, Prilla was safely on the ground. She had finally decided to undo the belt and hope that she could start flying before she hit the ground.

Luckily, she was quite high up, and this wasn't a problem.

That was a close one! Prilla thought. She would have to be more careful in the future.

Now she needed to find the butterflies again. Where could they have gone? Prilla decided to visit Lily's garden. All those fruits and flowers would be certain to attract butterflies – or so she thought.

But as she flew over the garden, Prilla saw that she was wrong. There wasn't a butterfly to be seen.

Lily saw Prilla hovering overhead. She put down her hoe and waved Prilla over. Prilla cupped her hands around her mouth and called down to her friend, "I can't stop now! I'll be back later!"

Lily nodded and went back to work. How Prilla envied Lily. She got to spend her day doing what she loved most!

Prilla took a sharp turn and headed to Marigold Meadow. She saw many fat honeybees but not a single butterfly. Next she went to the spot where the sweetest bunch of clover in all of Pixie Hollow grew. But there were no butterflies there, either.

Puzzled, Prilla landed and began to search more slowly. She peeked inside hollow logs. At one, she startled a chipmunk family. They chattered at her angrily. She lifted cabbage leaves to search underneath them. But she found only snails, which quickly scooted into their shells. She looked inside cool dark caves. She even searched among the long grasses that grew near the shoreline. She saw a crab shell and a piece of pretty blue beach glass. But there wasn't a single butterfly to be found.

Prilla sat down and leaned against the hollow shell. *It's almost as if they're hiding from me,* she thought. Then she laughed. What a silly idea!

She closed her eyes for a split second. Without even thinking about it, Prilla blinked over to the mainland.

What fun! She was in a nursery school class with dozens of children. She flew into a castle that a girl was building out of blocks. Prilla waved to the girl from a turret. Then she flew over to two boys who were each pulling on one end of a teddy bear. Prilla got their attention by doing loop-de-loops in the air. The teddy bear fell to the ground, completely forgotten.

Prilla was heading over to the doll corner when she felt someone shaking her shoulder.

"Prilla, are you okay?" a familiar voice asked.

7

PRILLA LOOKED AROUND. She was sitting on the ground. Her hands were behind her. And – *Oh dear*, Prilla thought – Pluck was back. She was looking at Prilla anxiously.

"Are you okay?" Pluck asked again. Her brow wrinkled in concern. "Oh – were you blinking to the mainland? Did I bother you?"

Prilla shook her head. "It's fine," she said.

"I found the blackberries!" Pluck said proudly. She held up a basket filled to the brim with three berries. "Would you like one?"

Prilla nodded. Pluck held out a big juicy berry. But as Prilla tried to reach for it, she discovered something very odd indeed. She couldn't move her hands. They were stuck together behind her back!

This is strange, Prilla thought. She struggled mightily. Her hands wouldn't budge. *Could they be tied together?* she wondered. *But how? And why?*

Pluck continued to hold out the berry. An annoyed frown started to form on her face. Prilla couldn't explain her predicament to Pluck, since she herself had no idea what was going on. But she knew that it would be rude not to take a bite of the berry since she had asked for it. Not knowing what else to do, Prilla opened her mouth like a hungry baby bird.

Pluck's expression changed from annoyed to puzzled. She held the berry to

Prilla's mouth. Prilla bit into it. The juices dripped down her chin.

"Delicious," Prilla said, trying to act as if eating like this was completely normal. She took another bite. "Mmmm."

When Prilla had eaten her fill, Pluck quickly said good-bye. She headed off toward the Home Tree with the remaining berries. *Pluck will have an interesting story to tell when she gets back!* Prilla thought with a giggle. *She must think I am very odd indeed!*

After much struggling, Prilla was finally able to slip her wrists free. She discovered that they had been bound with thick threads of spider silk. *How did that happen?* Prilla wondered. *Did some spider mistake me for an extralarge fly? Was I about to become a spider's next meal?* That was a scary thought! She had never heard of a spider capturing and devouring a Never fairy before. But she guessed that anything was possible.

Well, no use worrying about what could have happened, Prilla thought. She was safe and sound, at least for the moment. But what an odd day she was having!

Prilla took a deep breath, closed her eyes, and made a quick wish. "Please let me find the butterflies," she said.

She opened her eyes and looked around. Nothing. If only wishes came true that easily! But they don't – not even in Pixie Hollow.

She starting walking again, looking in all the usual places that a butterfly might choose to hide in. She looked in knotholes in trees, under dead leaves, in between rocks. Then she spied a flash of colour from the corner of her eye.

Prilla ran forward and peeked into the tall grass. There sat a butterfly. It was the tiny silvery yellow creature that she had chased earlier.

Prilla smiled widely. She felt incredible relief.

The butterfly opened and closed its wings slowly. It was so close that Prilla could see every colorful scale on its wings. It was so close that she could reach out and...

Her movement startled the butterfly. It took off, then landed a couple of inches away.

Prilla sighed in frustration. But then she was surprised to see the butterfly turn around. She quietly crept up to it. But the butterfly wouldn't stay put. It flew a short distance, then landed, flew a short distance, then landed, over and over again.

They went on like this for quite a while, Prilla following closely. Once, she lost sight of the butterfly. Her heart sank, and her eyes started to fill with tears. But then it reappeared right in front of her. It was almost as if the butter-fly had been looking for her.

Suddenly, the butterfly flew away into a thicket. Prilla ran up and parted the leaves. She hadn't lost it after all this, had she?

To her surprise, she had discovered a small clearing. And there were the butterflies – all fifty of them!

Prilla grinned. *Take it slowly this time,* she told herself. *Try not to make any sudden movements that will startle them. Everything is going to be all right.*

Just then, Prilla felt a tickle in her nose. *Oh, no! I can't sneeze now,* she thought. *That will scare them away again!* She wrinkled her nose to make the itch go away. She held her nose, but nothing worked. What was wrong with her?

Then she noticed the leaves on the bushes around her. She was standing right in the middle of a patch of sneezewort!

*Ah-ah-ah-*CHOO! Prilla sneezed so hard, she nearly knocked herself over. *Ah-choo, ah-choo, ah-choo!*

Finally, her sneezing fit ended. Prilla was not surprised to find that she had scared the entire butterfly herd away –

again. She backed away from the sneezewort patch. Noisily, she blew her nose into a leafkerchief.

Prilla shook her head. What bad luck she was having!

8

PRILLA'S STOMACH RUMBLED. She had been searching for the butterflies for quite a while, and she was awfully hungry. It was time to eat her breakfast.

Spotting a table-sized toadstool, Prilla landed next to it. She began to unpack the food that Dulcie had given her that morning. She was pleased to find two strawberry muffins, a clay thermos full of hot tea with honey and lemon, and a cobweb napkin. Prilla sprinkled some fairy dust on a smooth, round stone. She floated it over to the toadstool table for a comfortable place to sit.

Just as she was about to take a seat, a breeze blew her napkin off the toadstool.

She bent to pick it up.

Prilla straightened, poured herself a steaming cup of tea, and –

"Hey!" she said. "Where did my other muffin go?"

Had she accidentally knocked it off the toadstool? She knelt down to look for it. But the missing strawberry muffin was nowhere to be found.

She stood and reached for her remaining muffin. But it was gone, too!

Prilla was puzzled. This was too odd. Pixie Hollow was a place of magic and whimsy. Strange things happened every day. But strawberry muffins didn't sprout legs and walk away. There had to be an explanation.

But try as she might, Prilla couldn't come up with one. She poured herself a cup of tea. Then she settled down on the stone and took a sip. Her stomach rumbled again.

Looking around, Prilla spied a raspberry bush nearby. "I'll just have a berry for breakfast instead," she said.

Splat! A big juicy raspberry landed right on the toadstool table. Red juice splattered everywhere. Prilla jumped to her feet, spilling her tea. *Now, where did that come from?* She looked up at the sky. *A passing bird must have dropped it,* she thought.

"Lucky it didn't hit me on the head," she said out loud.

Splat!

Berry juice dripped down Prilla's face and onto the collar of her dress. She had spoken too soon!

She wiped the sticky juice from her forehead and cheeks with the cobweb napkin. *Unless I want every wasp in Pixie Hollow to be buzzing around me, I'd better get to Havendish Stream and wash this off*, she thought. She placed the cork back into the thermos, put the thermos in her sack, took a step forward – and promptly tripped on a pebble.

How odd, thought Prilla. *I didn't see that there before.*

Shrugging, she slung the sack over her shoulder and headed for Havendish Stream. "What a strange day," she said. "It would be funny if it weren't so… " Then she started to laugh despite herself. It *was* pretty funny that so many things had gone wrong!

Prilla got to the stream. She knelt on

the bank, scooped up some of the clear, cool water, and splashed it on her face. She couldn't resist magically making a fountain or two spring up from the water when she was done washing. *I'm getting pretty good at this*, she thought. *Rani would be proud.* Rani was the water-talent fairy who had taught Prilla how to make fountains. *Maybe she'll let me move on to water creatures next! I bet I could make a sea horse!*

Smiling at the idea, Prilla raised her head and began to straighten up. And there, on the opposite bank, sat a blue and golden butterfly. Prilla blinked. The butterfly fluttered its wings two or three times, then took off into the air.

Prilla was right behind it. She hoped the butterfly would lead her straight to the rest of the herd.

She followed the butterfly along the banks of the stream. She trailed it through an underground passage. She chased it around and around a big oak tree until she was dizzy. She followed it past the Mermaid Lagoon… and ended up right back at Flower Field.

If I didn't know any better, Prilla thought, *I'd think this butterfly was taking me on a wild-goose chase!*

At the edge of Flower Field, the butterfly suddenly darted under a pile of dead leaves. Prilla landed nearby and slowly crept up to it. She stifled a giggle as she saw the leaves rustle. The silly butterfly thought it was fooling her!

Prilla lifted the top leaf.

This is a surprise! was all she

could think.

For there was no butterfly under the leaf. Instead there was a Never stinkbug – an angry Never stinkbug. It *was* a surprise – and a particularly unpleasant one at that!

The stinkbug raised its tail, and – *whoosh!* – it drenched Prilla from head to toe in its horribly stinky perfume.

"Yuck!" cried Prilla. She stepped back, coughing.

As she wiped the tears from her eyes, she glanced up. Sitting on the branch above her head was the butterfly she had been chasing. Its wings were shaking. Prilla could have sworn that it was laughing at her.

9

THE BUTTERFLY FLEW OFF, but Prilla didn't follow. Instead, she sat down and put her head in her hands. She was stinky, sticky, and worn out. Maybe it was time to give up. It was quite clear to Prilla that she was a terrible butterfly herder. She had no idea what she was doing. She was starting to dislike butterfly herding – and butterflies themselves – very much.

Then again, if she gave up now, the herd might get lost, or harmed by predators. And it would all be her fault. Prilla couldn't bear the thought.

I can do this! she told herself. She stood up and began to retrace her steps.

When she returned to the spot where her muffins had gone missing, to her surprise she spotted a butterfly. It was a pretty pink and bronze one. It sat there sunning itself on the toadstool she had used as a table.

The butterfly's back was to Prilla. Smiling, she slowly began to creep up behind it. She was careful not to step on a dead leaf or a twig. She didn't want to make any noise that would scare the butterfly away. *This is my last chance*, Prilla thought. She had to catch this butterfly!

Finally, Prilla was right behind the creature. She took a deep breath and lunged forward to grab it. "Gotcha!" she yelled.

The butterfly froze. Then it toppled over.

Prilla stared. Her mouth hung open in disbelief. She reached over and softly poked the butterfly's wing with her finger. It didn't move.

No doubt about it. The butterfly was dead.

"What have I done?" Prilla cried. She took a deep breath. "Oh, why did I pretend to like butterflies in the first place?"

Once again there was a flash of purple, and Vidia landed right next to Prilla.

"Hello, precious," Vidia said with a smirk. "I've been looking for you all day. How's the butterfly herding going?" She wrinkled her nose. "And what is that awful smell? It smells like... ugh – stinkbug! Prilla, what in Never Land have you been up to?"

But Prilla was too upset to reply. She

slowly raised her arm and pointed to the motionless butterfly.

Vidia looked at it, then turned to stare at Prilla. She wore a look of shock. "Precious, it's not… ?"

"Dead," finished Prilla forlornly. "Yes. I killed it!"

"My goodness, sweetheart," said Vidia. "Now you've really done it. Even *I've* never killed a butterfly."

This did not make Prilla feel any better. "I must have scared it to death," Prilla whispered.

Vidia shook her head. "You know, this never would have happened, darling, if you had just – "

Prilla put her hands over her ears. "I know, I know! But I can't think about that now. Will you please go get Queen

Clarion so I can explain everything to her?"

Vidia raised an eyebrow. "Are you sure, dear?" she asked. "You could just pretend this never happened. I won't say a word."

Prilla was aghast. "No, Vidia! I must tell the queen."

"Suit yourself, precious," said Vidia. "I'll be back in two shakes of a dragon's tail."

Prilla watched as Vidia took off into the air. Then she lowered herself to the ground and leaned against the toadstool, where the tiny butterfly lay still. She could hardly stand to look at it. She closed her eyes and dropped her head into her hands. What a disaster this was! She wasn't a butterfly-herding fairy. She was a butterfly-slaying fairy!

After what seemed like a lifetime, Prilla heard Vidia and Queen Clarion approach. She was surprised to see that Nettle was with them. *Maybe she's been brought along for an expert opinion,* Prilla thought. With all the butterfly herders sick, caterpillar-shearing-talent fairies were the next best thing.

Prilla wiped her eyes and stood up.

Nettle opened her mouth to say something. But Prilla held up her hand for silence. "Please let me speak," she said. "I have a confession to make, Queen Clarion. Something terrible has happened and it is all my fault."

"Go on, Prilla," said the queen.

"I... I.... I... killed a butterfly." Prilla lowered her eyes in shame.

"What butterfly? Where?" Queen Clarion asked sharply.

"Here," said Prilla, pointing to the toadstool. But when she turned her head to look, she was shocked.

The butterfly was gone!

10

"B-B-B-BUT IT WAS JUST HERE a minute ago," Prilla stuttered. She turned to Vidia. "You saw it. Tell her!"

Vidia gave her a wicked smile, which made Prilla even more upset. She turned to the queen. "It's true! It was just there!"

"What did the butterfly look like?" the queen asked.

"It was pink and bronze," Prilla said. She was trying hard not to cry. "It was very small... "

The queen burst out laughing. "Perhaps it looks like the butterfly that is sitting on your head?" she asked.

Nettle started laughing, too. Vidia shook her head, smirking.

Could it be true? Prilla reached

up. Sure enough, there was a butterfly sitting on her head like a jaunty little hat! It took off into the air and landed on the toadstool. It was the very same butterfly Prilla thought she had startled to death.

"But how… ?" Prilla began.

"Oh, Prilla," said Nettle, catching her breath. "Don't you know that butterflies like to play practical jokes?"

"What are you talking about?" said Prilla.

"They'll do anything to play a trick on you," Nettle explained. "One time a butterfly carried away my best pair of shears. And the next morning, all the caterpillars had terrible haircuts!"

"And there was that time a herd of butterflies picked up a sparrow man who had fallen asleep in a patch of clover,"

Queen Clarion added. "They took him to one of the highest branches of the Home Tree. He was horribly confused when he woke up later, high above the ground."

"But this is the meanest butterfly trick I've ever seen," Nettle told Prilla. "Imagine, it pretended to be dead so you'd think you had killed it."

"It *was* a good joke," Vidia said. She liked mean jokes.

Prilla stared at the other fairies. She couldn't believe what she was hearing. "That can't be right," she said. But then she started thinking about the day's events. Getting stuck on the twig. Having her hands tied up with spider silk. The sneezewort. The missing muffins. The berry that fell on her head. Tripping over the pebble. The stinkbug attack.

And this – the butterfly that played dead.

"I can't believe it! So *that's* what's been going on all day," said Prilla. She was so relieved, she started to chuckle.

Nettle and the queen gave her puzzled looks. "But you love butterflies. So why didn't you know about them?" Nettle finally asked.

Prilla stopped laughing. It was time to tell the truth. "I–I–I told a lie," she admitted. She was too ashamed to make eye contact with anyone. She stared at her shoes as she spoke. "I said that I liked butterflies. But the truth was that I didn't really like them at all. And I didn't know a single thing about herding them. I still don't!"

"But why did you say you liked butterflies?" the queen asked.

Prilla gulped. She began to explain how at first she had felt honored when other fairies asked her to help out with their talents. And how, after a while, it had begun to take time away from her own talent. But she had been afraid to say no to the fairies who needed her.

Prilla turned to her friend. "Nettle, to be honest, I don't really like shearing caterpillars. I'd rather blink over to the mainland. I didn't want to hurt your feelings. So I pretended that I liked butterflies."

"Prilla," said Nettle, "you silly fairy. I love my talent. I think you're crazy for not liking it, too. But I would never want you to do something you didn't like."

"Yes," said the queen. "Prilla, you can be an honourary whatever-you-like talent in your spare time. But Pixie Hollow has only one mainland-visiting clapping-talent fairy, and we need you."

Vidia snorted. "Imagine liking butter-flies! Didn't you think something was odd when no one else would volunteer?"

"Not even animal-talent fairies like working with butterflies!" Nettle added. "They're one of the only creatures they can't communicate with."

Prilla nodded. She felt embarrassed and happy and relieved all at once. Then she noticed that the pink and bronze butterfly had landed by her feet. She looked at it affectionately. Sure, the butterflies had made her life difficult. But they were beautiful creatures. And they really didn't mean any harm; they were just… mischievous.

Perhaps she didn't hate butterflies after all.

Prilla took a step toward the butterfly. Immediately, she sprawled out on the ground. The sneaky little butterfly had tied her shoelaces together!

There was a moment of embarrassed silence. Then Prilla started laughing. Queen Clarion and Nettle joined in. Vidia crossed her arms and gave Prilla a mocking look.

And the butterfly? It was laughing, too, of course!

No, Prilla thought, shaking her head. *I definitely do not like butterflies one bit, that is for sure!*

Join Tinker Bell, Prilla and all
the other Never Fairies in
the next Disney Fairies book...

A Masterpiece
for Bess

Here is a fairy-sized preview
of the first chapter!

A
Masterpiece
for
Bess

"EVERYBODY! COME TO MY room!"

Tinker Bell flew about the tearoom.
In a silvery voice she called out to the
fairies and sparrow men gathered around
the tables.

Lily and Rosetta, two garden-talent
fairies, looked up from their breakfast of
elderberry scones.

"What's the hurry, Tink?"
asked Lily.

"Bess has just painted my portrait –
and you've got to come and see it!"
Tinker Bell urged.

Rosetta and Lily looked at each other
in surprise. It wasn't every day that Bess
painted a new portrait! What was the
occasion? they wondered. But before they
could ask, Tink had darted out the
tearoom door and into the kitchen.

"Let's go," Rosetta said to Lily. They
followed Tink through the Home Tree up
to her room.

There the fairies packed themselves
in wing to wing, like honeybees in a hive.
They could see Bess, in her usual paint
splattered skirt, standing at the front of
the room. She was hanging a life-size, five-
inch painting of Tinker Bell.

"Isn't it amazing?" gushed Tink. She

flew up behind Lily and Rosetta and landed with a bounce on her loaf-pan bed.

And indeed it was. Bess's painting was so lifelike, if a fairy hadn't known better, she might have thought there were *two* Tinks in the room. No detail – from the dimples in Tink's cheeks to her woven sweetgrass belt – was overlooked. What Tink loved most about the painting, though, were the gleaming metal objects piled all around her: pots, pans, kettles, and colanders. She felt as if she could almost pull each one out of the painting.

It was a perfect portrait, as everyone could see. Right away the oohs and aahs began to echo off the tin walls of Tink's room.

"It's lovely!" said Lily. "Bess, you've outdone yourself again!"

"You're too kind. Really," Bess said. Her lemon yellow glow turned slightly tangerine as she blushed. As Pixie Hollow's busiest painter, she was used to praise. But she never tired of hearing it.

"It's just what Tink's room needed," added Gwinn, a decoration-talent fairy. She gazed around Tink's metal-filled room.

"What's the occasion?" asked Rosetta.

"Oh, no occasion, really," said Bess. She brushed her long brown bangs out of her violet eyes. "Tink fixed my best palette knife, and I wanted to do something nice in return."

All around her, the fairies murmured

approvingly. Bess felt her heart swell with pride. *This is what art is all about,* she thought. Times like these made her work worthwhile.

"Personally, I don't see what the fuss is for," a thorny voice said above the din. "Honestly, my little darlings, what's so great about a fairy standing still?"

Bess didn't have to turn around. She knew who the voice belonged to – and so did everybody else. Vidia, the fastest – and by far the meanest – of the fast-flying-talent fairies, came forward.

"Oh, Vidia," Tink said with a groan. "You wouldn't know fine art if it flew up and nipped you on the nose."

"Yeah, don't listen to her, Bess," Gwinn called out.

"It's okay," Bess assured them. "Every fairy is welcome to have her own opinion."

But as she looked at the portrait again, she frowned slightly. It wasn't that Vidia's criticism bothered her. She'd learned long ago to let the spiteful fairy's snide comments roll off her wings like dewdrops. But Vidia's remark had started the wheels in Bess's mind turning.

"You know… ," Bess began.

She searched the room for Vidia. But the fairy had already flown away.

"'You know' what?" asked Tink.

Bess shook her head. She turned to Tink with a sunny grin. "There's a whole day ahead of us!" she said. "I don't know about you fairies, but I've got work to do."

Spreading her wings, she lifted into the air. "Thanks for coming, everyone," she called.

And with a happy wave, Bess zipped off to her studio.